Creating an Inviting
Classroom Environment

by
Elizabeth S. Foster-Harrison
and
Ann Adams-Bullock

Library of Congress Catalog Card Number 98-65081
ISBN 0-87367-633-5

This fastback is sponsored by the Suffolk County Chapter of Phi Delta Kappa International, which made a generous contribution toward publication costs. The chapter sponsors this fastback in memory of James V. Fogarty, Sr.

9177208

Table of Contents

Introduction

Readers of this fastback will find many suggestions for teachers, administrators, and parents about how to make a school better by improving the physical environment. We have spent two years analyzing environmental features that seem to make a difference to students and teachers (and to parents). This study has offered us an opportunity to respond to attitudes and preferences that often are overlooked in public education but rarely neglected in the business world. The result has been an honest look at what matters to people about the environment in which they work and learn. How a school looks does affect how everyone who goes there feels about it — and about what goes on inside it.

While circumstances usually prohibit teachers from changing the entire school, they can and should make a difference in their own classrooms. We have identified several important things that any teacher can do to make his or her classroom environmentally friendly.

Some environmental features do not affect the classroom directly but can affect students' and parents' first impressions of the school in general. Thus we also provide suggestions for administrators that can help their schools make the best first impression.

Sometimes older school facilities seem like "lost causes." But even a modest makeover can improve the environment. And for schools still on the drawing board, we detail critical features that all educators and parents should review before building begins.

The physical environment of a school and its classrooms plays an important part in the support and ownership that a community will feel toward the school. Our hope is that readers will find the information in this fastback interesting, current, and practical. This work represents what we believe to be an important view into what the people who pay taxes for schools and those who work or learn in schools would like to see.

Creating an Inviting Environment

Jenny told me last night that she really likes her new school. When I asked her why, she said, 'It's just not like a hospital — like all sterile, you know, where everything is white and untouchable. We can sit on the floor and learn and it's O.K. I really like that.' "

This was a conversation between a mother and a daughter that was repeated by the mother a week after school started. The mother said that Jenny, who recently transferred into a fifth-grade class from another school, was very happy with the new environment. The mother was interested in why Jenny liked the school. She commented throughout the conversation on how "warm" everything seemed and how welcomed she and other parents felt. What engenders such feelings?

Just Good Housekeeping?

We begin by looking at two classrooms. The first is a seventh-grade language arts/social studies classroom. The door to the classroom usually is closed. There is no outside room number or teacher name to identify the room or its occupants. When one enters, a first glance reveals that all of the desks are set in straight rows facing the front, where a traditional blackboard is the focal point. The walls are painted white, and the floor is light-brown vinyl flooring. On a bulletin board to the right of the door hang curled sheets of information, a newspaper clipping or two from several weeks earlier, a fire escape-route diagram, and the daily bell and lunch schedules. The bulletin board is not covered with any paper; the cork shows around the pinned-up papers.

To the left of the door a list of classroom rules is taped to the wall. Above the center of the blackboard are some pull-down maps and a pull-down projection screen. There is a world globe on an old table. Windows fill the left side of the classroom; they are covered by venetian blinds with several broken slats.

The teacher's desk is strewn with students' papers and four stacking trays, a grade book, attendance book, and seating chart. Bookends hold up a dictionary, the faculty handbook, and teacher's editions of texts used in the class. The overhead projector in the front of the room has noticeable wear; heavy-duty tape holds the projection arm onto the machine. A traditional hand-crank pencil sharpener is screwed to the back wall, just above one of two computers that sit on a long table. One computer has a dust cover over it; the other does not. The uncovered computer has a sign on it that says, "Use Only With Permission." But on that sign is a Post-It note that says, "Out of Order." The one bookshelf in the room holds about 75 paperback books with a few out-of-date magazines stacked on top.

A big "Welcome" sign, banners, and other decorations can help make students feel good about coming to school.

While this classroom description may seem exaggerated, unfortunately it is altogether too common in many schools. The second classroom provides a contrast:

The door of the second classroom is partly open. Above the door is a classroom number. On the outside of the door itself is the teacher's name on a brass-colored plate. And on the wall to the right of the door is a handmade welcome sign with a list of the homeroom students' names on it.

The flat-top desks have individual moveable chairs. The desks are arranged in groups of four to facilitate different types of group work and student production. Three walls are painted a soft blue color, and the fourth

11

is covered with wallpaper. One section of the room features an accent color applied primarily to the window frames and door moldings. A variety of colorful posters on the walls relate to language arts. In the back of the room there are a set of globes and a storage cabinet where different class sets of laminated maps are stored. The blackboard is constructed in two parts; one half is for traditional chalk, the other is chalkless and requires dry-erase markers.

There are two large bulletin boards in the room. One is to the right of the door and is divided in half by a wallpaper border. One half is labeled "School and Team News"; the other half is "Current State and World News." This bulletin board is covered in a light yellow paper with the information sheets pinned on top. A second bulletin board is in the back of the room and is used for interactive instruction. Activities for a unit about Asia are placed there.

Large windows covered by miniblinds and topped by a colorful valance fill the left side of the room. Placed neatly on the teacher's desk at the back of the room are a name plate, a vase of fresh flowers, and three small, framed photographs of family members. It also holds a stack of books related to the Asia unit. Behind the desk is a small bookcase that holds more pictures, mementos from a recent trip, an art print standing on a small easel, and two brass bells.

Two working computers are in use, and above them are posters with directions and other information, including sign-up sheets. A long table stands ready for student projects and holds a small wicker basket of colored markers and pens, an electric pencil-sharpener, and three stacked plastic bins of scissors, glue, and small squares of construction paper. An area rug marks off a reading area containing an old rocking chair and two beanbag chairs.

Classrooms such as this second example also exist in many schools. Most people — teachers, students, parents — tend to view the second example as the better environment. But does the classroom environment make a difference in achievement or performance? Is it worth the time, money, and effort to create an inviting environment such as the one described in the second example? We believe the answer to both questions is "yes."

Reasons to Focus on Environment

It is not difficult to identify a variety of factors that affect how students feel about a classroom environment. Following is a sampling of available information that supports the need to consider many aspects of climate in order to create an environment for maximum learning:

- Environments that are psychologically or emotionally negative inhibit learning (Midjaas 1984).
- Fewer students in a larger instructional space enhance the use of available resources. Spaces where high density and few resources exist add to increased student/teacher conflict and poor student-to-student behavior (Midjaas 1984).
- Quality classroom light is conducive to 1) greater comfort and contentment; 2) a more cheerful envi-

ronment; 3) more concentration and a greater desire to work; 4) less fatigue and therefore fewer side-effects of fatigue, such as laziness, bad posture, nervousness, and lack of interest; and 5) greater accuracy and neatness (Hathaway 1983).

- Teachers who have less need for a position of control will locate their desks in positions of less visibility (Arends 1994).
- There is no clear-cut relationship between the noises associated with school (such as group work) and student performance on task (Arends 1994).
- Studies have found direct correlations between students' cognitive styles and responsiveness to environmental characteristics. In responsive classroom environments, students' achievement increased (Dunn and Dunn 1992).
- Reading speed and accuracy increase when students are allowed to have water and snacks (MacMurren 1985).
- An animal companion program, developed in a school with 15 at-risk sixth-graders, resulted in a lower incidence of fighting at home and school, increased respect for adults, and improved grades (Meek 1995).

Age of buildings shows no significant association with attendance, behavior, academic achievement, or delinquency. The difference among buildings on these characteristics has to do with imaginative and well-planned use of decorations for the school, according to Rutter, Maughan, Mortimore, and Ouston (1979). The more successful schools appear to be "smart and well cared for." Following is a sample similar to the preceding list, but which focuses on aesthetics considerations, such as color and decoration:

- Decoration and care of school classrooms are associated with higher student achievement in secondary schools. The use of posters, plants, and pictures in the classrooms have shown to have a positive effect on student behavior (Rutter, Maughan, Mortimore, and Ouston 1979).

- Use of blues and greens fosters feelings of relaxation. Use of red and orange colors in instructional areas induces anxiety behaviors (Weinstein 1981). Color affects changes in mood, emotional states, psychomotor performance, muscular activity, rate of breathing, pulse rate, and blood pressure (Hathaway 1983).

- Students and educators prefer home-like features and surroundings to help interpret daily living at school. Examples include: clothes closets rather than lockers, ruffled curtains in windows, old-fashioned screen doors, soft places to sit, live plants and flowers, pets, attention to decorating details, food smells from the cafeteria, hooks for aprons, and pictures and trophies hung on walls where they can be touched, instead of stored behind locked glass cases (Meek 1995).

Comfort, including how classroom furniture is arranged, is another important factor. Again, the following list provides a sampling of available information:

- The feeling of warmth can be added to a room through the use of yellow and rich brown colors in furniture, bulletin boards, and carpets. In addition, low ceilings, 10 feet or less, with incandescent lighting or soft, warm table lights in small, individual work areas increase the feeling of warmth. Feelings of coolness can be created through use of blue, green, pale neutrals, and white; by keeping floors bare; and by high ceilings. Lights should be fluorescent and the room quiet with optimum ventilation and sparse furnishings. Keep the design of school furnishings straight, plain, and basic (Hathaway 1983).
- People hear better in a brightly lighted room than in a dimly lighted one (Frohreich 1986).
- Achievement increased in high school English and reading, middle-level mathematics, and elementary reading when flexible seating arrangements were used in the classroom (Hodges 1985).
- Schools that display students' work tend to have a somewhat better level of success on exams (Rutter et al. 1979).

Decor with a Purpose

The purpose of the preceding lists is not to say that classrooms should be decorated with ribbons and bows, but rather that attention to the environment for teaching and learning is both necessary and proactive. Teachers have a right to work in a professional-looking environment that facilitates, rather than hinders, what they do. An appealing work environment should be expected; teachers should not be apologetic about wanting to work in an appropriate space.

More important, students also have a right to study in an environment that is conducive to mental concentration, physical activity, and other learning processes. Secondary students spend some 150 hours in a given classroom each school year. Elementary students, who do not move from classroom to classroom, can spend between 900 and 1,200 hours in the same room each year. Time in school, in a classroom, and on task can be enhanced by attention to teachers' and students' physical surroundings.

Stimulating, aesthetically pleasing classrooms and other areas of a school also encourage feelings of community. A sense of community, along with appropriate instruction, can help students succeed. And a "friendly" school environment is more likely to attract parents and other community patrons who can be important partners for successful schools.

Attention to the school and classroom environment — decorating with a purpose — goes beyond making a space "feel good" to its occupants. Numerous studies, in addition to those already cited, suggest that purposeful attention to the learning environment can improve both teacher and student performance, attitude, and motivation. Teachers and administrators may look at their own schools and ask, Is this facility too old to improve? Or is this space too small? In fact, size and age are not factors when creating an environmentally pleasing classroom or school. Newer and larger are not necessarily better. What counts is how the space is used, decorated, and maintained.

Perceptions of Environment: Study Results

Over a two-year period (1995-97) we conducted research on classroom environments in rural, suburban, and urban settings. Through observations, interviews, and surveys, we made comparisons between what teachers actually have in their classrooms and what they say is important to have in the classroom learning environment. We also compared this information to what students and parents think is important for an environmentally friendly classroom.

Our first task was to identify five categories for comparisons:

1. *Furniture* included any item that held students, teachers, or implements related to study or instruction. Examples are: storage chests, podiums, desks, chairs, filing cabinets, bookcases, and rockers.

2. *Aesthetics* identified decorative items in a classroom or school. The use of color, room arrangement, and special personal touches, such as photographs or mementos, are components of this category.

3. *Comfort* categorized items in a classroom or school that were there to provide "comfort," such as a reading center in which items are placed for students' comfort. In such a center, for example, four straight-back chairs would be negatively identified with comfort. However, large floor pillows, rocking chairs, and bean bags would by positively identified as comfort items.

4. *Instructional items* referred to materials or objects necessary for instruction; televisions, chalkboards, overhead projectors, and books would be some examples in this category.

5. *Professional items* were identified as artifacts of professional accomplishment, such as diplomas, certificates, awards, and recognitions — most of which were framed items hung on walls.

Three groups — teachers, students, and parents — were asked to rank characteristics within the five categories and separately to rank the five categories themselves by level of importance to the teaching and learning environment.

Results from Teachers

More than 400 teachers in grades four through eight in 38 public schools were interviewed and surveyed. We found a number of distinct differences between the "real" (what actually was in teachers' rooms) and the "ideal" (what teachers believed should be in the classroom). In a majority of classrooms, we observed (ranked by frequency): 1) bulletin boards, 2) various types of student desks, 3) televisions, 4) personal items of the teacher, and 5) other AV equipment (such as VCRs).

When we interviewed teachers, however, the items they believed to be most important for the "friendly" classroom included: (in the instructional items category) 1) computers, 2) television, 3) class libraries, (in aesthetics) 4) use of color on walls, and (in comfort) 5) flat-top student desks.

Only one item in the top-five "ideal" ranking, televisions, was consistently found in teachers' classrooms. Of the five categories, teachers ranked instructional items as the top priority for an environmentally friendly classroom and professional items as the least critical factor.

More than 125 teachers at the high school level (grades nine through 12) also were surveyed. These teachers, representing all content areas, concurred with their elementary and middle-level colleagues in stating that instructional items are the most important of the five categories in the classroom. The most important item in the school, consistently listed across grade levels in the aesthetic category, was a clean, neat building. Other important items were ranked: 2) a pleasant office staff, 3) room numbers, 4) teachers' names on doors, and 5) directions to the office posted.

In the furniture category, teachers concurred with students that the type of student desks greatly influences the friendliness of a classroom, and they ranked it number one in this category. Factors tied for second in the furniture category were comfortable reading furniture and storage areas for students' belongings. The aesthetics category produced a predictable number-one choice: a clean classroom. Also considered important (tied for second) were wall murals, use of color, and welcome signs.

Teachers classified manual temperature control as the number-one factor in the comfort category. They also said that open space (second) and windows that open (third) contributed to the environment. In the instructional category, the top five items at the high school level were: 1) the chalkboard, 2) technology, 3) bulletin boards, and tied for fourth place, evidence of student work in the classroom and manipulatives for teaching.

For the professional category, teachers ranked having their own desk in the classroom and their name on the door as the top two choices. In this category teachers also identified phones in the classroom and availability of professional journals among the top five choices.

We believe that teachers have the right to work in a professional environment. The results of our research indicate that giving teachers a few amenities in their environment can make a difference in how they feel about the environment and how they approach working in that setting. It would be unthinkable in a business environment for a professional to do without a phone, appropriate furniture, or important resources. But teachers do so every day. It is essential that more consideration be given to the environment in which teachers work, if schools want to attract and retain capable, competent individuals into the education profession.

Results from Students

Students in grades four through eight also were asked to rank the five categorized areas and specific choices under each area. We surveyed 775 students. These students ranked the comfort category as the most necessary to an environmentally friendly classroom, followed by the instructional category (for grades four and five), furniture (for grades six and seven), and aesthetics (grade eight). In the furniture category, students in grades four to six ranked student desks and storage as the top two items. Seventh-grade students said comfortable reading furniture and student desks were important, and eighth-grade students chose desks and comfortable reading furniture.

All five grades ranked a clean classroom as the most important factor in the aesthetics category. Other items consistently listed in the top five choices across grade levels were: use of color on walls, wall-to-wall carpeting, and such decorative items as posters and flowers.

Students in grades four and five ranked animals and technology (a tie) as the number-one instructional item. Students in grades six through eight listed televisions as number one. Other choices in the top five were bulletin boards and learning centers.

In grades four through eight, students ranked access to a phone as the number-one professional item that teachers need in a classroom. The second-ranked factor was teachers' names on doors.

High school students in grades nine through 12 also ranked comfort as the most important category of the five. But when asked for the top five most important individual choices, student responses differed among grade levels. Freshmen said that access to phones and teachers' names on doors were most important (perhaps because they do not know their way around the building). Sophomores, juniors, and seniors all agreed with their teachers that a clean, neat building was the most important item. Ranked second by all grades was access to phones. This choice tied with several others: pleasant office staff, teachers' names on doors, and a landscaped yard. Clearly the protocol of identifying rooms and associating them with people is an important point for all students.

Students in grades nine through 12 agreed that comfortable furniture and clocks in the classroom were the top two furniture necessities for a friendly classroom. They also ranked the type of desks (third) and storage available for their personal items (fourth) as important. Use of color in the classroom was ranked by all grades as an important factor for an environmentally friendly classroom.

For comfort, students felt temperature control, access to music, snacks, and water contributed to an effective environment. All high school students agreed with their elementary peers that television was the most important instructional item. Access to technology and the use of bulletin boards also were seen as important. Students in grades 11 and 12 ranked animals as important instructional items.

The three top professional items were phones (first in all grades), teachers' names on doors, and displayed diplomas.

Students' wants and needs in the classroom environment are different from those of the teachers but not to a significant extent. The importance of comfort, as the number-one categorized choice by students, should not be overlooked. According to many learning styles theorists, allowing students to choose comfortable seating and to be in a study setting that provides appropriate light and temperature contributes greatly to their willingness and ability to focus on important learning tasks.

Results from Parents

Parents also see comfort as the most important category for the environmentally friendly classroom. Parents tend to believe that their students' academic performance and behavior can be enhanced or diminished by the quality of the school and classroom environments. Specifically, parents believed that computers, learning centers, and student work on the walls positively affected academic performance. Parents included television in the instructional category as commonplace and expected.

They also listed several items that they believe affect student behavior, including:

comfortable reading furniture
live plants
use of color on the walls
student work on the walls
animals
computers
access to music
use of manipulatives for reading
learning centers
team log

classroom library
television
manual temperature controls

From Results to Recommendations

The preceding section reported the results from our surveys of teachers, students, and parents. From this information we can make the following recommendations in the five categories that we studied.

Furniture

Everyone surveyed saw classroom furniture as important. We recommend:

- Providing flat-top desks and chairs that can be separated or moved together for various teaching strategies. Ideally, both desks and chairs should be adjustable.
- Developing a "comfort" space with casual furniture, such as bean bags, big pillows, an old couch, or a rocking chair. Colorful material and paint can spruce up old furniture.
- Designating a space for student storage, either assigned desk storage or a separate storage area. Stackable crates and screw-in hooks are great alternatives if students share their desks and have no place for coats, book bags, and other personal

things. Lockers often are inadequate, particularly if they have to be shared or are stacked two or three to a vertical column.

- Hanging a clock in the classroom if one is not provided. Awareness of time helps students to better structure their work.
- Keeping the teacher's desk and related furniture away from the student traffic area to ensure that students have ample space for movement. The focus of a classroom should be on students and their activity spaces, not the teacher and his or her desk.

Aesthetics

For decor with a purpose, we recommend:

- Hanging seasonal or special event flags outside or inside the room, and changing them regularly. A smaller, mailbox-type flag can save money and still create interest.
- Painting classroom walls a light, bright color. Accents can be provided with contrasting colors for woodwork or wallpaper borders.
- Draping windows or using miniblinds to give the room a more home-like appearance. A window valance can dramatically change the look of a room at very little cost.
- Adding murals to focus attention. A talented local artist (perhaps a parent) or students can be enlisted to create the mural.
- Using floor coverings that "soften" the room both visually and acoustically. Carpet and rugs absorb

sound and increase the visual warmth of the class-room.

- Displaying a few personal items. Family pictures, travel mementos, and art prints show a teacher's human side.
- Providing live plants adds a sense of well-being and also can fill empty spaces well. Hanging plants, such as vines, are nice for windows and wall space that will accommodate the brackets; flowering plants are a double delight.
- Adding a welcome sign outside the classroom door. A consistent positive response seems to come from students and parents when they see welcome signs.
- Eliminating dust. All survey respondents mentioned cleanliness as important; therefore, efforts should be made to keep classrooms clean — and students can take a hand in the effort.
- Including an aquarium in the classroom. Therapists, doctors, and dentists often keep aquariums in their waiting rooms because of their calming effect; aquariums also are useful in science.
- Using seasonal decorations to add a festive air. Holidays can be highlighted, but other times or events, such as a community festival, also can be noted with balloons, banners, or pennants, many of which can be made by students.

Comfort

Thinking about the body and the senses — touch, sight, sound, smell, and taste — are important for comfort. We recommend:

A colorful flag and pleasant landscaping can make the school an inviting place for students, teachers, and parents.

- Providing manual control for classroom temperature.
- Regulating the different types and brightness of light. Facility planners and maintenance personnel

should consider light sources and color and use bulb covers to reduce intensity when necessary.

- Playing background music when students are working independently or in small groups.
- Arranging the classroom to accommodate different activities and to provide space for movement. Clustering desks can increase walking space.
- Providing a snack time for students. Many teachers now encourage students to bring nutritious snacks to class or to keep water bottles on their desks.
- Creating visually appealing and comfortable reading areas. At the elementary and middle school levels, such areas can have tents, lofts, hammocks, fluffy animal pillows, small stools, director's chairs, lawn furniture, air mattresses, rocking horses, area rugs, or other items.
- Using colors that create a mood of calm. Most experts advise staying away from reds and oranges, except as accent colors.

Instructional Items

Teachers ranked instructional items as the most important category in the classroom environment. While all classrooms have some common instructional items, each content area has specific items that teachers will need and want to use. Among the general items, we recommend:

- Incorporating technology, particularly computers for student use. Televisions equipped with VCRs are everyday essentials.

- Developing learning centers that include, according to their purpose, such items as music, audiotaped books, manipulatives, writing materials, and so forth.
- Adopting a classroom pet, both for its instructional value and as a "comfort" item. At the elementary level, teachers focus on needs and care of the animals. Older students will study relationships of animal species, survival needs, and life cycles.
- Developing a classroom library, which may mean asking for donations (either money or books) from parents.
- Displaying students' work. This single item showed up on all of the parents' surveys.
- Creating colorful bulletin boards that relate to instruction. These can be done by students or volunteers, who should work to make the boards interactive and content- or skill-specific.
- Using manipulatives, visual aids, and other sensory guides to help guide instruction.
- Designating storage space for instructional items and for materials created by students.

Professional Items

While there is much talk in the education community about teacher professionalism, this category was consistently ranked last in importance by teachers, parents, and students. However, in order for teachers to be seen as professionals, the teacher work environment must look like a professional workplace. Thus we recommend:

- Hanging framed diplomas and degrees on the classroom wall.
- Installing a telephone in the classroom and creating a directory of classroom telephone numbers.
- Providing a door nameplate and a room number sign.
- Using business cards for teachers (not just for administrators).
- Developing a directory in the school foyer that lists teachers' names and room numbers.
- Creating a "wall of fame" for certificates that students in the class have earned.
- Displaying an events calendar.
- Ensuring that equipment is in working condition and ready for use at all times.

Developing an Action Plan for Change

We address this section directly to teachers who have read the preceding information: Are you convinced that some modification of your classroom would improve relationships and environmental welcomeness? If so, then we offer the following, step-by-step advice:

Step 1: Look at your current classroom. Identify the items in your room that meet the criteria for improving the environment. List the things that should stay (though possibly be moved). Then invite a colleague or team member to your classroom to do the same thing and compare notes in order to make a final checklist. Students also can give suggestions.

Step 2: Think about and identify your own teaching style. The purpose is to match your preferences with the needs of the learners.

Step 3: Use the list from Step 1 to add items or characteristics that need to be changed or enhanced, based on your thinking in Step 2. This creates the blueprint for your environmentally friendly classroom.

Step 4: Create a budget and timeline for completing the change.

Step 5: Determine funding sources and partners who would be willing to assist you. Following are potential sources of assistance:

PTA/PTO	Class fundraisers
Civic groups	Auctions and yard sales
Corporate or small business sponsors	Teacher grants
	Volunteers
Wish lists for parents	A white elephant sale
Donations (money or goods)	University partnerships

Step 6: Implement the plan. Check off each item as it is completed.

Conclusion

Like many readers of this fastback, we have taught in all types of classrooms — some large, some small; some old, some new. We know the difficulties with slim budgets and declining resources in the face of increasing demands on time, money, and human energy.

The purpose of this fastback is to help educators respond to the whole child: the child who learns better when listening to music, the child who feels more relaxed surrounded by light blue walls, the child who needs movement and can concentrate better in a rocking chair. We can create the mood, the ambiance, the climate supportive of positive feelings and appropriate learning. It should be a part of every educator's plan to create the most positive and impressive classroom that will captivate and hold students' minds.

Teachers also deserve a clean, bright, and inviting place to work. These are not something that only "other" professionals deserve.

We know that in a community that opens its arms to newcomers and supports its residents through the care of its lands, parks, schools, and businesses, there are more innovations, more community civic awards, greater citizen involvement, and a deeper respect for the dignity of community members. Snapshots of such communities show positive activity and camaraderie. The practice of developing beautification projects throughout a district highlights the value its populace places on community pride.

It is no small coincidence that areas associated with lower socioeconomic status are less highly developed in terms of school support. They are more likely to have nondescript schools and other buildings in which broken windows go unrepaired and yards, where they exist at all, go uncut.

In the classic movie, *The Wizard of Oz*, Dorothy left dull, black-and-white Kansas for the colorful land of Oz, where she would travel the Yellow Brick Road. What wonder filled the eyes of the film's first viewers when the movie magically changed from black-and-white to color! Schools, too, can be in dull black-and-white; or they can be transformed with "color" in terms of attention to furniture, aesthetics, comfort, and instructional and professional items.

And what wonder will fill the eyes of students when they work and learn in classrooms that are focused on providing the best possible — the friendliest possible — environment for study. Teachers also will be delighted by the professional environment that such attention can engender.

Resources

Arends, R. *Learning to Teach*. New York: McGraw-Hill, 1994.

Dunn, R., and Dunn, K. *Teaching Elementary Students Through Their Individual Learning Styles: Practical Approaches for Grades 3-6*. Needham Heights, Mass.: Allyn and Bacon, 1992.

Frohreich, L.E. "Inservicing Teachers and Administrators on Classroom Environment?" *CEFP Journal* 24, no. 2 (1986): 10-13.

Hathaway, W. "Lights, Windows, Color: Elements of the School Environment." *CEFP Journal* 21, no. 3 (1983): 33-35.

Hodges, H. "An Analysis of the Relationships Among Preferences for a Formal/Informal Design, One Element of Learning Style, Academic Achievement, and Attitudes of Seventh and Eighth Grade Students in Remedial Mathematics Classes in a New York City Junior High School." Doctoral dissertation, St. John's University, 1985. *Dissertation Abstracts International* 45, 2791A.

MacMurren, H. "A Comparative Study of the Effects of Matching and Mismatching Sixth-Grade Students with Their Learning Style Preferences for the Physical Element of Intake and Their Subsequent Reading Speed and Accuracy Scores and Attitudes." Doctoral dissertation, St. John's University, 1985. *Dissertation Abstracts International* 46, 3247A.

Mann, Larry. "Designing the Learning Environment." *Education Update* 39 (September 1997): 1, 3-5.

Meek, A., ed. *Designing Places for Learning.* Alexandria, Va.: Association for Supervision and Curriculum Development, 1995.

Midjaas, C.L. "Use of Space." In *Instructional Leadership Handbook*, edited by J.W. Keefe and J.M. Jenkins. Reston, Va.: National Association of Secondary School Principals, 1984.

Rutter, M.; Maughan, B.; Mortimore, P.; and Ouston, J. *Fifteen Thousand Hours.* Cambridge, Mass.: Harvard University Press, 1979.

Weinstein, C. "Classroom Design as an External Condition for Learning." *Educational Technology* (August 1981): 12-18.